We Are Not an Error But the Idioms of Our Era

We Are Not an Error But the Idioms of Our Era

Poems by

Ndaba Sibanda

© 2023 Ndaba Sibanda. All rights reserved.
This material may not be reproduced in any form, published,
reprinted, recorded, performed, broadcast,
rewritten or redistributed without
the explicit permission of Ndaba Sibanda.
All such actions are strictly prohibited by law.

Cover design by Shay Culligan
Cover image by Ntokozo Mhlanga
Author photo by Sipho Ndebele

ISBN: 978-1-63980-359-0

Kelsay Books
502 South 1040 East, A-119
American Fork, Utah 84003
Kelsaybooks.com

Contents

My Growing Interest Is in a Forest

What piques your interest
when you walk into a forest?
Its interrelated patterns, aura?
Its processes, fauna and flora?
Its fertility and biodiversity?
Its leafiness, calm and novelty?

I see diverse plants like I detect our cultures
For forests are home to 80% of land creatures
Plants cover 31% of the world's total land area
Trees push out pollutants, give us scent hysteria
Greenery ably absorbs greenhouse gas emissions
What a slight, chaotic tree cutters are temptations!

Did I mention that a billion souls depend on forests
for their incomes and daily subsistence requests?
40% of global renewable energy is derived from
forests. Where do medicinal properties come from?
Talk of wood, solar, hydroelectric and wind power,
of leaky, teary trees; revel & feel the flood devour!

Increasing the Resilience of the Disadvantaged

I sing a serious song in support
of our naturally rich ecosystems
that are delicate and vulnerable,
that call for action, for defense.

I sing a serious song in support
our lovely natural environments,
of the need to protect biodiversity
and deepen resilience of poor groups.

The Magic of Working Together

The crucial meeting under a huge tree
brought together a number of villagers,
environmentalists and community leaders.
Touching on the importance of working
together, one naturalist used an example
of two companies working together for their
mutual benefit and growth: *synergy is the concept
that the combined value and performance of two
establishments will be greater than the sum
of the separate individual parts. in other words,
interaction or cooperation gives rise to a whole greater
than the simple sum of its parts. Similarly, whether
some of you is a hunter or cuts down trees for wood
for fires to heat up one's home or to cook food,
or to build houses, or to clear land
for agricultural use, we just have
to work together in harmony
with nature and one another.*

My Recent Read

I read of a funding freeze
on coal-fired power projects
since the planet seeks to shift
away from the polluting fossil fuel.

I also read of a partnership in Zambia—
the launching of a plastic neutrality project
aimed to lower plastic pollution in that nation.

The Land Held Lovely and Legendary Stories

The muse had vanished for a long time. It had.
Where's the muse?—she whined and wondered.

The land was very pregnant with unborn stories,
it was in labor in a wing of untold, unsung tales.

Scratchy stories were held under the tongue
of Mother Nature, words rioted in Bongi's mouth.

Like rabbits crawling out of their caves and holes,
words searched for their release and their voices.

She wanted to get unstuck in order to do what
she cherished, she desired to torch her knack.

She craved to explore the majesty and loveliness
of our delicate and deprived planet, Mother Earth.

She had plumbed into the depths of the bendy rivers
and listened to their sweet songs and sweaty snarls.

Rains had purified and drenched her on several occasions,
hissing snakes and animals gave her a sense of adventure.

She who had conversed with tall trees, picky and perfect peaks,
for nature and its valleys and all held stories she itched to tell.

Not in Recorded History

Deadly droughts drained
and bubbled because of
a ferocious flash of furore

Let loose were temperatures
That made the world fierier
than at any time in noted history

Seas acidifying, species on the brink
of death, the earth barked a bitter welcome
To an unwelcoming upheaval of heat and hell

A Global Obligation

one of the demanding crises
of our time is the responsibility
to protect the earth's precious lands
and seas, for human beings have a duty
to tackle the biodiversity and climate crisis

Fleeing by Virtue of Poisoned Air

Sleepless, helpless and hopeless souls,
they stalked sanity as pastoral victims.

They sought to scurry away from the perils
of soot pollution. They just could not breathe.

Susceptible and underprivileged communities:
children and the elderly members were escaping.

Had they not had enough of the threat posed
by soot air pollution? Was it not a health hazard?

They pursued to ditch poisoned areas where souls
griped over asthma, respiratory and heart conditions.

Fee-Free Facts and Thoughts on a Tree

You are a plant that captures sunlight and provide
a day's supply of oxygen for me & for three other souls.

Tree, you store carbon dioxide in your fibers in order
to help us clean the air, you are the lifeblood of upkeep.

You do not only contribute to the environment by providing
oxygen, you also benefit health by catching dust & pollutants.

You do not only boost health, but also enhance wildlife
by offering a home and food to birds, fungi & insects.

You merit a high-five since you improve the environment
& slow the rate of global warming by absorbing carbon dioxide.

You support the soil, beautify the land, scent the air,
stimulate my soul, stop soil erosion & flooding.

Tree, I cannot think of posterity, prosperity, peace
& spirituality without thinking of your value and role.

For you improve air quality, outline climate betterment,
boost water conservation and soil preservation in style.

Tree, your preservation is our health, my happiness,
our future, our worth and a huge part of our world too.

A Canopy of Charming and Cheery Stars

an author is a soul who seeks a time
to reflect on one's observations and all,
a 'wow' weekend of harmony and happiness,
a retreat from the typical world to the untypical
one of words that irradiate, renovate and recenter,
an atmosphere of fullness, friendliness and fun,
a community with a cornucopia of cordiality, care
and creativity, a perfect experience of possibilities,
and opportunities where one engages in chats
with oneself, where one basks in the sunshine
by the serenading stream, fantasies and falls
asleep under a canopy of charming, cheery stars.

Nature Needs Peace

Woes of wars include human injuries,
causalities and massive physical demolition
of the environment and the infrastructure.

The act of severely destroying the environment,
ecocide, toxifies the soil, adversely affects the earth,
as plants and the forests are inevitably shattered.

We Are Nature

tell me, how do we rescue ourselves
from our propensity for self-destruction?
from self-hatred, self-delusion, self-infliction?

an investment to save the natural world
is a welcome development to save life,
for we are inseparable from nature

wetlands are no longer wet,
for humanity has become brutal,
no longer loving, caring and romantic,

do we see the trees' tears
when we tease and hack them
for no reason or for the fun of it?

do we hear the poor animals' pleas
when we pester and poach them
for the love of money, meat and abuse?

do we appreciate the importance of trees?
do we recognize the damage of tossing
litter around, or plastics around beaches?

rainforests are unfriendly, furious and fiery,
coral reefs are quarrelling with extinction
because life's support systems are stressed!

nature is glory and glory is nature
but nature calls for regeneration,
determination, not decimation

trees, rivers and oceans cry foul,
they say their ruin is our tragedy,
indiscriminate tree-cutters, heed!

there is no place for plastic polluters,
for plastic pollution is harmful to humans,
animals and plants as it affects the food chain

is the protection of the planet
not the protection of the people?
is a bulge of natural ruins not enough?

a sick planet dogged by polluted air, water
and soil, struggling with floods, fires, hunger
and starvation: global warming is real and scary

please poachers and polluters,
precious is life, fragile is our planet,
we plead on the edge of extinction

all peoples should be preservers,
put our planet before pride and greed,
deforestation, devastation, extinction

are we ready to consume less, use less water,
upcycle more, turn trash into treasure, compost
food scraps, shop secondhand, walk, bike, not drive?

The Drones and Designs of Our Time

pen, please pay attention
for a while, I beg of you,
this ode has to be birthed,

let you and I curate and compose
an ode to our pained, puzzled planet,
to the peoples of this worried world,

let this piece find meaning in a meaningless
era, humanity in the face of inhumanity,
love and hope in a loveless, hopeless kiss,

to the protagonists, present and prospect,
let it be a work of poetry of our time, a song
to jog our memory about ecological onuses,

pen, please play your role,
is it time to pamper our egos
with honeyed words that are void?

is it time to paint our pride, pranks
and poison with a galaxy of sugary stars?
to perpetuate retrogressive progress?

can nations move beyond speeches, promises
and pledges and deliver on their promises,
and feel for those on the frontlines of this crisis?
please, delve into Africa's development
issues, discuss climate change challenges
and the impact of the COVID-19 pandemic

how can Africa escape prolonged food
insecurity in the face of climate change?
how can there be climate change justice?

does climate change not seek to decimate
and incriminate peace of mind and ecosystems?
are its effects and ire not looking us in the face?

can the climate change crisis be tackled
without a candid talk on justice and funding
for the most vulnerable for a livable future?

pen, please please us with valor
and vigor versed in vicious verities,
for in our vicinity love should dwell,

pen, please paint personalities
with proper brushes, proverbs,
prints and purrs of our time

time is a tool too priceless to fritter away,
it's time to deal with our scars and stains,
not to denounce and destroy the ricochets

that bare but not beautify the blemishes,
pen, please pour over all, worthy or shady,
admit our feats, fears, frailties and faults

The Story of Our Lives

The story
on the state
of the world
reignites his
reading ritual—
it torches a fierce fire
in his soul, in his heart,
his mind wonders & races
after the mysterious variants
that are causing nothing else but
mayhem and misery across the world,
he rebukes: stop this archaic hide & seek
game, how can you change the rules of the
match in the middle of the game? this isn't
entertaining, fair & sharp, it's cruel, variants!
that's why Heartlessness is your . . . first name
& nickname, Mulishness is . . . your surname!

Forsaken floods & wildfires, & other disasters,
I puncture your tireless tire with a powerful prayer!
for our planet & its peoples need peace & progress,
I see more & more conservationists, editors & scribes
contribute to the action and activism on climate change.

a work of art
that explores
the greater snags
the global village
faces on a daily basis
especially the climate
change crisis and the corona
virus . . . paaaa . . . pandemonium,
oh . . . my confessions . . . pandemic!

A Poet's Prophecy Is Potent

a poet's vision transcends boundaries
of time, distress, despair and devastation,
of pettiness, pretenses and pampered pranks,
It carries counsel, it breathes fury and fun,
Overt or veiled, it should be the voice
of intention and action, of the people
as it discerns democracy from dishonesty,
Decency and development from decay,
It draws strength from its invincible wings,
It is an invisible and unstoppable messenger,
Yet it strides with caution and determination,
It is a witness to the unleashing of humanity's
Worst instincts, tyranny, immunity and greed,
It's nobler for it to writhe on the thorns of realities
Rather than to thrive on delusions and deceits,
It stings suppression with its teeth of freedom,
It brutally bites bigotry in the bums and bones,
It ruptures lies and hoopla with facts and figures,
a poet's prophecy cannot be thwarted by threats,
a poet's revelation discerns and descends on rot,
a poet's voice should not be drowned by rumpus,
But be imbued with lucidity, love and loveliness.

Time to Change Course

it needs more protectors
than pretenders, polluters,
it's pulverized by polluters,
precious planet is pestered,
nature is no longer nurtured,
species are enraged and endangered
for two-thirds of the rainforest is ruined,
human life reduced, the coral reefs halved,
will the look of mass extinction galvanize
the wealthy nations to turn half of the world
into a great, green zone, a reserve for nature?
lovely oceans, rivers and trees scream for care,
please people, the planet has to be protected
from unkind and destructive human activities,
for a wounded natural world is a hurt human life

Climate Change Calls and Africa's Needs

The realist called them CCC, an acronym for
Climate Change Calls, sweet-sounding words
In the face of a man-made climate change crisis

The claimant claimed he would supersonically cut
The use of fossil fuels, of unclean energy sources,
He talked about his wonder of the green energy,

The use of renewable energy sources:
Wind power, solar power and biomass,
Of net zero emission transport sectors,

Of cleaner technologies and electric cars,
But the pragmatist told him to balance the drive
For the green agenda with Africa's energy needs,

He reminded the claimant that the continent
Contributed least to global emissions yet is most
At risk from a heating planet, an ill-treated earth,

He pointed out that Africa struggles with energy
Poverty, with a number of Sub-Saharan Africans
Who have no access to a reliable source of electricity

Why It Sparkles and Wrinkles

My eyes marvel at it, I am charmed and absorbed
I cast light on its color, a healthy hue of freshness

It gifts me with a brightness bold, big and beautiful
My eyes feast on sepals, petals, stamens, carpels

Bloom, you chase away doom with your freshness
You fan me with your fantastic color, a brilliant breeze

Nature's gift, a source of food for other organisms
Blossom, bloom blossom, let your cool cologne flow

Nicely into nostrils, heal and hypnotize a soul
Sent to thrill and spill, no cent can buy that scent

Endowed with an eye-catching appearance
You withstand the pressures of pests, weather

Proper fertilization, post-harvest care are crucial
What a freshness, flower, you weather winds

Flower, I fell in love with your luster long, long ago
For the shine on you brightens the room of my heart

I love your lustrous leaves, peaceful petals, stylish stems
Vibrancy vibrates around your fine and firm buds and stems

They thirst for water and the warden's cup of wisdom and will
Sweet flowers, a scenery like heavenly decorations that delight

Flowers that sparkle are cared for via consistent quality control
One's good practice of planting, harvesting, post-harvest handling

It is it wise for flowers to wait and wait and yet wait for water in vain?

They wait till they start wailing "water woes are wars we can't fight!"

Flowers in poor quality wilt, wail, dance a dull, drooping, drowsy dance

High quality flowers speak a lovely language of fascination and freshness

Who Does That, People?

restrictions and protocols ruled,
I remember the cruel Covid days,
fears and tears swept across souls,
scary news bombed us, the old gave
in to the new but onto hope we held,
we became proficient at pondering
praying, prying, peering and masking,
some lost their jobs and peace of mind,
others fell into retirement as if to start
spending their dear children's inheritance,
I dived into literature and it gave me relief
and a window into the lives of other souls,
I dreamed of funny folk brushing up against
a season to reason, marching on a horizon,
of midair getting kindlier, calmer and crispier,
of cute crickets chirping in the oaks in the forest,
of nature chastising humans of being the worst
cooks ever in the world, after all, who bakes such
a dangerous dish of mess like climate change? I ask

No Climate Justice Without Financial Compensation

From 6–18 November 2022, the United Nations conference on climate change will take place in Sharm El-Sheikh, Egypt. There is talk of fostering of dialogue and exchange of ideas and solutions in a bid to achieve climate and development goals together, but mere talk without financial commitment and compensation for the poor communities and countries that have been forced to bear the brunt of this crisis will not bring relief and justice to the world's most susceptible souls. The summit takes place on the backdrop of persistent droughts, cyclones that have caused mayhem and misery to life and property, it takes place on a continent whose nations are clearly climate-vulnerable.

Bee's Bounciness

Bee's Bulawayo
upbringing is crucial
as she sifts through life's
precious pieces and paths
past where the storms make
landfalls and where mudslides
and floods and fires live and loom

A Day in the Life of a Birdologist

Ever wondered what it's really like to be a bird?
What do birds get up to in their day-to-day lives?
How do they spend their free time, if ever they have
such time? Flying, chirping, loving, laying . . . I hear
you murmur. Questions. Do all birds have feathers?
Yes. Do all birds fly? I am told a man once said that
all birds fly, and including "a specific type of birds
that makes a sound similar to that of an old car failing
to start." That particular group, though, not a *murder*
of crows, looked murderous because it simply didn't
take kindly to such an affront. Maybe humans should
learn how to talk and co-exist with birds and be polite
and careful. I repeat, that was not a *murder* of crows.
I heard that a weight of penguins growled, honked
and peeped in a murderous fashion. Poor innocent
birds! That cluster cried: *We swim. Not fly. Don't lie!
Get your facts right.* Oh, as if that weren't enough
unease for him, a rather rude rookery of ostriches,
emus, and kiwis was also up in arms. Talk of
having a bad day. Birds are beautiful. That riotous
raft gave him a rhetorical question. *Did you see us
fly high? Don't lie!*

How I wish I could invite all kinds of birds
on this attractive earth to share their many
& various experiences & give us the incredible
inside scoop! Because birds are beautiful. I can
hear the ostriches making an impassioned plea
to all persons on this earth: *Birds shouldn't
be provoked. For instance, we ostriches, have
powerful, long legs that can cover 10 to 16 feet
in a single step. Our legs can also be useful
and intimidating weapons. Our kicks can kill
a human or a potential predator like a lion.*

Forewarned is forearmed. Let's live in harmony.
During one of my nature walks, guess what happened?
Your guess is as good as mine. I saw lots of lovely trees,
insects, birds and animals. in a fruitful forest in Plumtree,
I bumped into a soul who had an expensive-looking camera.
That soul claimed to be a birdwatcher and a birdologist.
What? a birdologist? Possibly a university researcher?
Two little adjectives. Two little S's. I visualized them.
S*ophisticated* and s*tudious.* That's great for the future.
I imagined. I soliloquized. I exclaimed. That soul said:
*No, far from it. I'm just a simple observer who appreciates
& respects birds; my happy heart is rapt, reinforced
and reinvigorated by merely seeing, sensing, serving,
hearing and hanging out with them. It's transcendent.
I experience heaven on earth, the musicality and vitality
of the wild, the sanctity of life, the filmic majesty of nature,
the power and proximity of love, the perfection of creation
exposed in glory when birds are snoozing, chirping, chatting,
loving, laughing, napping, nuzzling, hopping, helping
feasting, flying, fooling, meeting and . . . yes, mating.*
The birdologist advised me: *If you seek full and expert
knowledge on why birds have great wings but hollow
bones, warm blood, an astonishing respiratory system,
a huge, strong heart; or to gain insight into their behavior,
physiology, and conservation and habitats, then perhaps
you should consider making a date with an ornithologist.*
Courtesy saw me applaud, thank & bide the birdologist.

Climate-Smart Farming

Farmers are talking business,
they seek to up their game
and be proactive, positive,
creative and productive,
and be ahead of the volatile
moods and swings of the weather
and automated inventions and all,
they seek to be thriving and content,
they will match the capriciousness
of the weather with their smartness,
they hope to export their produce soon,
hence their discussions center on best
practices on climate-smart farming
and that is sweet news to the ears
of the forex-hungry citizens and all!

Harvesting Happiness and Health in Bulawayo

urban gardening is a common feature of horticulture
in Bulawayo, a perennial dry region, there's a culture
of growing and cultivating vegetables and maize,
adapting peri-urban agriculture to the climate change maze!
residents water their plants during the night, they use improved water
harvesting strategies to boost borehole yields, for precious is rainwater,
in an edgy economy, urban farming plays a crucial nutritional, financial part,
forget fertilizers, pesticides, health risks: for the dwellers, these *workouts* are smart!

Eguswini Is Where He Is Restored

a man clad in creased khaki shorts and a shirt,
his eyes engrossed in the arresting thickness
of a tree, with its lovely luxuriant leaves,
barks and branches, his attention is seized
and swayed by the denseness of a forest,
and its various shrubberies and prairies
and vagaries of shades, scents and sounds;
a cute camera is snuggled on his chest,
insects, birds and all things wild in bounty
in attendance, in action and holding sway;
the man seems to be unbound and aired
and exhilarated by nature in its purest form,
an inhalation of happiness in a healing haven,
for nature nurtures and nuzzles a suffering soul,
nature sweeps away a sickness with its sparkle
nature releases, relaxes and revives spirits
he calls it Eguswini, a wonderful woodland
it is a sanctuary of saneness and freshness
maybe he is a naturalist, a birder, a hunter?
it could be he is saying birding is a bright shot?
the cicadas and birds are humming harmonies
perhaps he is an alert hearer, an observer?
happy birds, flowers and trees won't harm him,
all they seek is coexistence, pacific protection
possibly he is a birdwatcher, a conservationist?
without doubt nature is exultant and fragrant
its touch is priceless, profuse, pristine and perfect

Of Their Noises and Vocalisations

a parrot is pretty,
and probably prudent &
peculiar because it *talks!*

come to think of it,
the above stanza has five Ps,
perhaps a parrot says: *I'm a person?*

I wonder why a swan *cries*
while a snail *munches* & maybe . . .
maybe that's why a linnet *chuckles?*

How I wish I could see a rooster's
internal clock that makes it envision
sunrise, a day-to-day hunt for food

and of course, territorial protection!
a rooster *crows* a *wake-up* in the morn,
& the vim for its day & nightly crows?

a kangaroo *chortles,* as if to say,
your hearing, sight & hopping abilities
are not a patch on mine, you're game!

The other day I heard a kangaroo boast:
I can hop 25 feet, come in several sizes
& shapes, use my tail as my fifth leg!!

I guess it's not a wise idea to sneak
into a hideout with a flashy frog since
it croaks, & a petty pig that *snarls,*

but call to mind, it can tell you
how it is smarter than a dog
that *barks,* that it can't sweat!

why does a hyena *laugh?*
strange as it may sound, by virtue
of a sense of frustration & insecurity,

One day I said: enough of domestic noises
and vocalisations, because a horse was
neighing, a donkey *braying,* a cow *mooing:* moo!

a goat lowing: maa!, a dog *howling:* owooooooo!
a content cat *purring, meowing,* a duck *quaking,*
a *cackling* chicken after laying an egg, what a tune,

after saying enough of the *egg song,* I headed
for the forest, a mannerless mosquito tingled
me before buzzing & whining away, damn!,

evading my swat by the skin of its proboscis,
how could it bite me to obtain protein that
it needs in order to lay its eggs? more what?

that meant more mosquito bites in the future,
in the wilderness a quail *called,* a lion *roared,*
a hapless hare *squeaked,* a cricket *chirped,*

a monkey *chattered* like a tireless gossip,
so much so that an okapi let out . . . yes
a mocking, maddening *cough* while,

a giant alligator appeared & *bellowed,*
& if that did not get me crying & cringing,
the elephant's *trumpeting* saw my feet fly away!

Sleeping Rivers

Sleeping rivers keep secret what they harbor,
hide their fury's strength behind a placid face

Under their tongue lies an innocence, an obedience
that catches and cripples strongmen's tentacles

Sleeping rivers can drown the dross of dancing sharks
and unleash and flex muscles with an amazing depth

The waters of sleeping rivers—when stirred up—when
tampered with—breathe a fire which swallows up sharks

Come on Board the Sierra Leonean Plane

Where is the outcry or the urgent assistance from Africa?
are the Sierra Leoneans not dealing with a massive mudslide?
Where is the outpouring support from the international
    community?

Torrential rains gave birth to flooding and a colossal mudslide,
a patter of heavy rain reigned a trail and a terror of devastation,
People lost everything: lives and limbs and property and
    possessions.

Where is the outcry or the urgent assistance from Africa?
are the Sierra Leoneans not dealing with a massive mudslide?
Where is the outpouring support from the international
    community?

Remember Sierra Leone has had her fair share of challenges,
Recall she grappled with a stubborn civil war, then the Ebola crisis,
Now vulnerability is taking a toll on homeless mothers and
    children.

Where is the tangible solidarity and the spirit of unity from Africa?
are the Sierra Leoneans not dealing with a massive mudslide?
Where is the oneness of humanity from the global community?

People had the nightmare of wading through muddy waters,
They were submerged, buried under mud with their houses;
The survivors sought to dig up with their bare hands.

Where is the tangible solidarity and the spirit of unity from Africa?
are the Sierra Leoneans not dealing with a massive mudslide?
Where is the oneness of humanity from the global community?

Sierra Leonean survivors and rescue workers and others
Who have risen to the call of duty are overwhelmed,
It's time for the world to show greater solidarity.

Lessons from the DRC

Waiting for an international landslide victory
of support for the victims and survivors
of heavy rains in north-eastern
Democratic Republic
of Congo

Lake albert is gripped by mourning
Parts of a mountain caved in
People were submerged
Whilst their households
Were buried under

African governments should tackle
Heavy land deforestation
and avoid crowding
Groups of people
into sharp hillsides

Africa Still Haunted by the Land Quagmires

To transfer or not to? To compensate
or not to? To tackle them or to ignore them?

From forceful land displacement and dispossession
to land empowerment? To decongestion? Food security?

Land. The soul of the people. Elite capture of the land
redistribution? Land. Legislation? Constitution? Consultations?

Redistribution. Tenure. Restitution. Land expropriation.
Equity and justice? any sacred cows in the land reform issues?

We Need Us

We will need a convergence
of programs and persons
To make this city glorious again

We will need a convergence
 of expertise and experience
To set industries in motion

We will need a convergence
of funds and new research
Methods to deal with health

We will need collective efforts
To turn around the fortunes
of Africa and the world

Going the Natural Way

when the school holidays were in full swing
her body was ready for a roller coaster ride

be it food or drink or cohabitation or coition
Lisa flung herself at it like a ravenous sacrifice

but somehow, she was hurt and indisposed
she began to look at herself and her health

she sought some therapies and approaches
to health and healing and natural happiness

it was more than a rumpy or grumpy life
it was about self-healing of the mind

and the body and the spirit to flourish
on the pathway of optimal health

Citrus Farm

fruit is fun for sure
but what ensued
was fraudulent

when we were
young passing by
in a bus or a car

what we used
to marvel at
was your sight

what a spectacle
of lined greenness
singing production

the aroma of oranges
was stout and loud
in rich Esigodini

now there is the scary
odor of dying trees
crying redundancy

many a villager says
it is a sign of sabotage
others see betrayal

it stares us in the face
with sickening spikes
of shamelessness

dear citrus farm
please promise
you will not die

citrus fruit what
happened was silly—
suicidal tendencies

citrus fruit we all
long for your scent—
your great greenness

your juiciness we all
adored and extolled
as we exported you

can moldiness shape up?
or it should just ship out
for freshness to jet in?

citrus farm come back
with your greenness
to restore our richness

A Healing Heart

inner beauty is priceless
its twinkle is taintless
its hoot is humankind
its love is one of a kind

inner beauty is invaluable
its splash & sparkle, silent & able
it is an oak wood which is yielded
from the solidest timber ever preserved

in general, it provides trust, temperature
moderation & is prized for real furniture,
groundwater recharge, water pollution
attenuation & air pollution reduction

like an oak tree, its heart is harvested
& invested in humanity, it's cultivated
to weather moisture, rotting and decay
during different seasons & times, I say!

butted by lost winds & earths that are unclean,
inner beauty remains shiny, solid & evergreen,
it grows both in temperate & tropical climates,
a handsome heart heals medical ailments & mates

A Conservationist's Cough of Concern

as the environmentalist took
a tour, he thought about green
beauty in relation to the ugliness
of dead beasts, fishes, birds,
insects and leaves—lost lives;
his name was Jabu Mtshana,
as he caught sight of the debris:
the destroyed homes, he felt
a certain mass of sympathy
and pain pinch, weigh on him,
and he remembered how folks
used to probe, ask him whether
ecosystems shaped and served
as an agent of positive change
and regeneration and titivation,
he thought about prescribed fires
and how they support wildlife
by creating new habitat or
improving existing habitat;
but he looked around and saw
devastation, dismay and death,
wildfires had consumed it all—
wildlife habitat and timber, all gone,
the conservationist visualized
and sensed adverse developments:
an upsurge in air pollution, eye
and respiratory tract irritations,
coughing, nose and throat rage,
a decreased in lung function,
a rise in stress, soil erosion, floods
and landslides, a *climate change crisis,*
he saw losses of shelter, food, money,
ashes, hospitalizations, burns, injuries;

and an increase in carbon dioxide
into the sky, into the atmosphere,
and felt the tang, smell of wildfires;
he coughed, coughed and choked
on the swelling plumes of the smoke

The Grain Song

Lorraine, here's the domain of words slain,
I'm here to entertain, attain, not to feign!
Hop onto the train, you won't sing in vain,
Words can reach a fever pitch in a brain!
in another twist of drama, let me explain,
Grain, you remain her main food and gain
in spite of others' disdain, sprain and pain,
She doesn't consider you as a stain or a chain,
I see her pound you grain, again & again like rain,
What a drain, yet she doesn't refrain or complain.

A Woman at Work

Her brain is on the grain that is being prepared
and processed. There is no maze in a common
sight and sound as the maize grain is threshed
 and pounded by crude mortar and pestle.

She is grinding corn in a mortar. a mother of 5,
in a village where the mill is far, she has no
choice but to manually process all her grain.
It is a backbreaking, laborious chore.

She learnt the traditional principles of hulling
and milling when she was a little girl since
her parents couldn't afford paying for
commercial grain-milling services.

She knows the importance of food production,
the goal of milling: enhancing the digestibility
of the grain for human consumption,
to produce a grainy, palatable meal.

Her pestle weighs 4 kg and the pounding task
is sweat, toil, time and energy. It is an effort.
Mortar and pestle are a pair moulded
from a tree stump and branch.

Why It Sparkles and Wrinkles

My eyes marvel at it, I am charmed and absorbed
I cast light on its color, a healthy hue of freshness

It gifts me with a brightness bold, big and beautiful
My eyes feast on sepals, petals, stamens, carpels

Bloom, you chase away doom with your freshness
You fan me with your fantastic color, a brilliant breeze

Nature's gift, a source of food for other organisms
Blossom, bloom blossom, let your cool cologne flow

Nicely into nostrils, heal and hypnotize a soul
Sent to thrill and spill, no cent can buy that scent

Endowed with an eye-catching appearance
You withstand the pressures of pests, weather

Proper fertilization, post-harvest care are crucial
What a freshness, flower, you weather winds

Flower, I fell in love with your luster long, long ago
For the shine on you brightens the room of my heart

I love your lustrous leaves, peaceful petals, stylish stems
Vibrancy vibrates around your fine and firm buds and stems

They thirst for water and the warden's cup of wisdom and will
Sweet flowers, a scenery like heavenly decorations that delight

Flowers that sparkle are cared for via consistent quality control
One's good practice of planting, harvesting, post-harvest handling

It is it wise for flowers to wait and wait and yet wait for water in vain?

They wait till they start wailing "water woes are wars we can't fight!"

Flowers in poor quality wilt, wail, dance a dull, drooping, drowsy dance

High quality flowers speak a lovely language of fascination and freshness

When the Sky Turned Red

It ignited anxiety and alarm.
The sky turned into a red ether
as torrents and torrents of lava
gushed from Mount Nyuragongo.
as if it had been waiting for darkness
to creep in, lava spilled, spiraled and
shattered people's precious possessions.

The volcano eruption left a trail of devastation
and distress as homes were damaged, lives lost.
in the wake of the adversity, the evacuees wondered
about the whereabouts of their kids, relatives and friends.
as luck would have it, some reunited with their loved ones.
The displaced victims needed shelter, water and basic food,
not forgetting sanitation amenities and information and news.

A Revolution

the indigenous people's pleas
manifested themselves in diverse miens
they claimed to be estranged from their past
from their ancestral land, alienated and abused
isolated from their rich culture and their language
their voices were a rare revolution of language too

Relocation Promises and Problems

the government officials and the mining company people
displaced the villagers, including the small-scale miners
to make way for mining operations, they promised
the relocated villagers arable lands, grazing lands,
jobs, schools and a decent compensation fee,
but after being pushed away
from their ancestral lands
hopes are vanishing
as hardships linger
around their
livelihoods

what the displaced villagers battle with are few jobs,
insufficient accommodation, inadequate land,
living in fear for the lives of their children who
learn in makeshift classrooms, living in derelict houses
without clean water, living in fear of the ramshackle houses
crumbling on them while they are asleep, living in fear of losing
the houses as they do not have title deeds, no property security,
living in fear that they could be relocated again, living in fear
of a government that delights investors at the expense
of the local people, living in fear of uncertainties

On the Side of Sustainability and Sanity

humanity hailed noble efforts of visionary game changers
as countless countries—big or small, poor or prosperous—
declared that they were marching into a decade
of cleanness, decisiveness and determination
in a bid to decrease greenhouse emissions
and protect civilization, and pledged never
ever to be caught on the wrong side
of climate history

if it were a sunny funny fantasy
he wished he could romanticize on
and on, fondle and fertilize it on the spot
and dance for dreams sometimes come true

Happiness

She had been hounded, headbutted by strife,
Cheated by the moods, sparks & spins of life

Her challenges were many and various—spiritual,
occupational, environmental, mental and financial

She was named May since that was her month
of birth, but what evaded her life were funds

It was in the month of May that she set out
on a life-changing path and gave it her bout

She sought happiness, health and holisticism
in spite of a hail of hellish winds and criticism

It was a daring, deserved and dynamic stride
to wellness that saw her life enjoy a real ride

Her life realized and relished a love for oneself,
hence, she recovered her purpose in life, herself

Hers was a life metamorphosed into meaningfulness,
characterized by regular exercises and liveliness

and a balanced diet, a good sleep, a positive thought
and a holistic way to health that made her less distraught

No, No Stress Please, I Stress

It is far much wealthier than wealth,
It is a happy heart's bastion of health
in spite of life's immaterial irritations,
inconveniences and complications,
It enables one to shut out negativities,
and to accept rigors and eventualities.

Peace, inner peace is crucial, I stress!
a spirit *free* from the effects of stress,
Isn't *being at peace* healthy and ideal?
The mind operating at an optimal level?
Dealing with life's anxieties and loads
Does not always entail potent swords

If peace of mind were a seed, a bud
Wouldn't we plant it in our backyard?
and water it first in our pictorial yard?
For peacetime is a game of psychology
a head needs to cease hosting acrimony
Before it becomes a fortress of harmony

Peace of mind is a conscious application
That comes with humility, honesty & action,
We need to bow and listen to it from within
For peace of my mind's first port of call is within,
It is a dignified and cautious state of mental calm,
It is a deliberate state of emotional and spiritual calm.

The Villagers Gave It Their Best

they were united and resolute,
the native villagers spoke up,
their voices were the loudest,
they protested over the project,
their strides were the boldest,
they piled pressure after pressure
on the oil project planners and executives,
they said their fight was not against progress,
but against anything that threatened wildlife
since it is a recipe for climate calamity and chaos,
in spite of threats their tenacity was unshakable

The Future Is Here

Forests blanched and bawled:
We're being bullied and baked
by vehement and vicious wildfires
This isn't just about emissions and fires
Please save us, save our planet, your planet
Think about what your grandkids will inherit

When a Dawn Danced in a Day

the sun rose a royal rise
and beamed a smile wide and wise
its striking royal rays glided and glowed
over sleepy shrubs that had never been mowed

Purify and Placate My Soul

I recall when I asked you to be my juice,
elixir, honeybun, you said you are profuse

under the spell of your touch scent
I did not comprehend what you meant

honeybun, you taught me what sunburn
is, honey, I love how you punch heartburn

let me unlock your feats, your benefits—
as laudable gels are your byproducts

we all seek to stay happy and hydrated
water-dense, you can't be underrated

you help us detox, purge and flush out
impurities, as we take you after a workout

soothing like a careful, cool sweetheart
massaging like a caring, cleansing dearest

when one wants to keep the skin clear
and hydrated, they take you without fear

you don't only heal burns, there is a wealth
of proof that you boost oral and digestive health

you excite me as you inspire peristalsis to help pass
stool without hurt or hassle, you are in your class!

natural laxative, go on fixing fissures, treating the skin
aloe vera, you patch up puffy gums, sunburn, heartburn

you come to our rescue when we are constipated
your nutrients and benefits leave us captivated

The Idioms of Our Era

We are the idioms of our time, a huge cabinet
We belong together, to this earth, this planet

Why do we thrive in muddle and destruction?
Walk in the ravines of unease and corruption?

Like words whose meanings cannot be found
From the literal or dictionaries that are sound

Let us be the proverbs: our lives are short
Let no hate thrive or live or receive support

Lessons on climate change need to be inferred
From wise sayings, actions or so advised a nerd

A Crying Crumbly World

Deadly droughts drained
and bubbled because of
a brutal blaze of heatwaves

Let loose were heatwaves
That made the world fierier
Than at any time in noted history

Seas acidifying, species on the brink
of death, the earth barked a bitter welcome
To an unwelcoming upheaval of heat and hell

You Are Neither a Terrapin Nor a Tortoise

shy reptile, where do you dwell?
I scan your bony, leathery shell,
toothless horny beak, terrestrial,
trunk enclosing the head, limbs, tail

believed to symbolize wisdom, fertility,
steadfastness, perseverance, tranquility,
healing, time, water, nobility, civility, protection,
home and retreat, adaptability, transformation

aquatic, shy reptile, you coast coolly under water,
I see you absorb, sock up the sunshine on shore, drifter!
you transition back and forth: water, land as you lay eggs,
while dogs bark, fight, you don't bite or tug at others' legs,
how have you roamed the earth for nearly 220 million years?
land turtles can live up to 40 years, sea ones up to 80 years,
is it true that we, humans, are youngsters compared to you?
who teaches me to retreat to my shell? no to chaos . . . you!
your species spend most of their time in water, is that so?
and a number of your species have webbed feet, is that so?
you teach me how to endure the test of time, what an expert!
lovely land turtle, your sea cousins have flippers, right?
I saw your species, your water-loving cousins . . . terrapins!
they said while they live in swampy places, your cousins,
the tortoises, without webbed feet, are lovely land urchins

The Villagers' Plea

The written communication from the villagers
was: put the issue of climate change at the heart
of your agenda, fund biodiversity, protect life
on the planet, defend indigenous communities,
safeguard their rights, put their plight and blight
at the center of the global biodiversity discussions.

The Plight and Blight of Climate-Vulnerable Countries

in the face of a series of droughts,
the disturbing incidents of cyclones etc.,
a climate change summit was convened.

"I would like to see meaningful engagement
between governments and diverse entities"
or so said the conservationist at the summit.

She continued, "It's time to make a turnaround,
to turn farm waste into green energy, this summit
is an opportunity to chart out a bold way forward."

"It's time to take up the cause of climate justice and shape
and build a safe and sound future, to push for the protection
and financial compensation for climate-vulnerable countries."

The Sweetness of the Vic Falls

Devoted to highlighting the marvels of the falls,
To capture the imposing touch of the environment,
The romantic side of the milieu, its warmth & wonder,
a cordiality, a singularity, a beauty that's cosmic and mystic
Which affords lovers a feast of heavenly happiness & harmony,
a love affair being lubricated, energized, fired up & transformed,
Tree branches waving at them, cute cicadas cheeping & cheering,
The waterfalls cascading with a meandering, mouthwatering musicality

Ruinous Rains

Cloudbursts on steroids
and climate change gave
rise to calamitous deluges

A Hunger for Dignity and Equity

indigenous peoples' rights
to their lands and forests
in jeopardy, in the spotlight,
no environmental justice?
what is the cost of exploited
natural resources and the sad
displacement of the inhabitants?
is change on the horizon for the poor,
for the abused ladies, seekers of justice?

has the world started
to imagine new confines
of justice, love and peace?
ballooning social inequality,
increased exposure to poverty
and the persistent perils of covid-19,
both of which impact the citizens'
shared or collective capacity to save
money or to make economic progress,
where is the hunger for justice, equity,
the dignity for all? where are solid efforts
to safeguard and repair our ailing planet?

The Magic of Snowflakes and Diamonds

I take a rather slow move
toward the magic of the snow.
My fascination: the frozen and crystalline state
of water that falls as precipitation.

Having no clear idea of a crystal or crystalline solid
or the process of crystal growth or crystallization
or solidification.
However, clearly craving for a sight of crystal twins,
those that are often symmetrically intergrown.

They just grow on me. I marvel at common crystals
like snowflakes, diamonds and table salt.

It would be cool if I went more into a world
inside the flake, a new world, a place
that is essentially warmer than we imagine.

Oh, what magic!

Who Killed Cecil?

innocently lured off Hwange National Park,
shot at with a bow and arrow,
injured and confused then tracked down
and killed in cold
blood with a gun.

Surely someone somewhere has to account for this
horrifying act of cruelty and other poaching crimes.

Our History and Heritage

You have muddied the waters of
Our glorious history and heritage,
Where shall we hide our long tails?
Our nakedness is now a public feast

Our Ecologically Advanced Africa

Africa of today in the year 2090 has transformed remarkably
in the year 2018 the continent had noisy and air-polluting vehicles
a united, clean and progressive Africa looked like a pipe-dream
    then
It took a few committed Africans to realize the Ultimate African
    Dream!

Who could have thought that Africa, a continent mired in sleaze,
    wars,
disunity and disease could emerge out of the ashes and be a giant?
Now with industrial pollution and corruption conquered and
    buried,
ecologically friendly modes of transport are the order of the day.

Africa has finally taken control of its destiny as Kiswahili has been
    codified
and is now used as a common language across the continent. It has
    promoted
social, political, economic, cultural cohesion and growth. Not only
    does Africa
have a common currency, also intra-African trade and green belts
    are changing lives.

When it comes to etymology they study the history of Kiswahili,
    Zulu, Amharic, Hausa
and Arabic words, their origins and how their form and meaning
    have changed over time.
Most of them use these languages as official means of
    communication and business.
Previously marginalized African languages and citizens are being
    promoted and protected.

The naturally rich continent has risen and is now a force to be
   reckoned with in economics
It has realized that feat as it got its politics right: democracy and
   development being central,
Though it has more new nations, it is relishing unrivaled peace,
   patriotism and fiscal growth.
It is the citadel of tourism, technology, etc., and a master in
   beneficiation, not corruption!

Those Must Fall

Fetch your tools, let us march and avert further damage
Our gardens are under siege, their greenery despoiled
They are marching, moving en masse as they raid and ruin
They devour just about everything in their wake, in their path

Fetch your tools, let us march and avert further damage
These destructive pests have no shame, silly insect armies!
Look how they are active at night, attacking our crops and grass
During the day, wriggling, hiding under our garden rubbles!

Come, let us take a closer inspection of our plants and prospects
Look at the armyworm eggs, let beneficial insects feed on them!
Set our caterpillars on them, hashtag: harmful little predators
Tell our farmers to take to twitter and twit: armyworms—must—
    fall

Mlungisi's Whereabouts

Mlungisi was a fixer
a mender of wounds
a repairer of hope and love
His village's renovator and mentor
They called him a corrector and an actor

Mlungisi's last known artwork was a mirror
Held up to the landscape of his deprived village
It was a looking glass held up to their society too
Mlungisi was an acute chronicler of world crises
in a world of greed, Mlungisi preached altruism

in a world gripped by the uncertainty of climate change
He propounded a bold trajectory, a climate revolution
a world rescued from burning rainforests and melting ice
a world salvaged from carbon emissions, from dirty fossils
by an investment in clean energy, green technology and jobs

But Mlungisi's whereabouts are unknown to his rustic admirers
It has been months since he vanished from his run-down village
Village dwellers are restless for he used to visit the sick in hospital
and console them regardless of whether he knew them or not
Mlungisi's plays corrected and converted rascals into humans too

A Short-Lived Incursion into a Cave

as dusk set in he set out on his trip
in line with the orders and directions
of one local lady prophet and herbalist.

in one of her burping trances, she stated,
"Listen, I unlock the secrets of the universe,
the mysteries that defy logic and science."

The seer advised him to tread into a nearby cave
and tug any creature he finds by the tail before
sprinting out whilst touching his troubled body part.

He wondered what cave dwelling animals he would find,
as he entered, he discovered that humidity was high due
to low evaporation rates, oxygen levels were low as well.

During the day the entrance zone usually receives sunlight
but it was already shrouded in complete darkness as if he
had reached the deep cave zone—which is the deepest part.

The true cave dwelling animals, the troglobits live in the deep zone.
in the dark he drifted and strained his eyes and guess what—came
across an accidental, a visitor or an animal that seeks a brief shelter.

Was it a real person? If so, was the person running away from a predator?
Was he or she a speleologist? Was he looking at a wandering ghost?
When the shadowy thing edged toward him, he shrieked and sped away!

Why They Called Her Ms. M

She was a hungry, pushy and predatory kisser.
She didn't like flowing water. She just didn't.
Do you know who she was? Ms. M. Her name.
She was fond of people who were too lazy
to empty their kids' wading pools. Those
were her victims too. She also adored
those who were too lazy to change
the water in their birdbaths.

She had no kind words
for those who kept the grass well-trimmed.
She resented them. She frowned at those
who walked in wooded or lush areas
while wearing long sleeves
and trousers. How dare they!
If ever one used an insect repellent,
then one was Ms. M's
downright antagonist!

She fed on plant nectar
and water. She was no innocent kisser,
not at all. Ms. M was a maddening
and toxic kisser. She kissed one
and left one writhing and reeling
from a stinging sensation.

Where did the kissing lady live?
Well, she lived in grasslands
close to areas where folks lived.
Stagnant water was her much—
loved breeding ground,
her happy habitat.

Together with her friends,
they gathered in storm drains,
they boogied in abandoned birdbaths,
in blocked rain gutters, pools and ponds.

Do you know what she did?
Well, Ms. M kissed Mr. Dube.
How did she do it? She pierced
Mr. Dube's skin and fed on his blood!
Ms. M bit him, injecting her saliva
into the old man's body while
draining off his blood. That
was no romantic kiss too.

I think bloody Ms. M was a vampire.
a bloodsucker. Mr. Dube felt the result
of her sharp kiss: a revealing red puffy bump.
Pain and itching held him hostage. Mr. Dube
whined as the bump became itchier, larger,
redder and stiffer. He developed body aches,
a headache, and fever. Ms. M was unworried
and unavailable to respond to questions
on why her saliva carried bacteria,
parasites and viruses.

Ms. M had left an itchy welt behind.
Bloody Ms. M! What a stinging sensation.
Squealed Mr. Dube seeking medical attention.

The doctor talked about vaccinations
and medications. The specialist said
"M stands for Mosquito. at home,

once bitten, treat mosquito bites
by washing them with soap
and water or pain relievers
or other anti-itch
medications."

A Woman at Work

Her brain is on the grain that is being prepared
and processed. There is no maze in a common
sight and sound as the maize grain is threshed
and pounded by crude mortar and pestle.

She is grinding corn in a mortar. a mother of five,
in a village where the mill is far, she has no
choice but to manually process all her grain.
It is a backbreaking, laborious chore.

She learnt the traditional principles of hulling
and milling when she was a little girl since
her parents couldn't afford paying for
commercial grain-milling services.

She knows the importance of food production,
the goal of milling: enhancing the digestibility
of the grain for human consumption,
to produce a grainy, palatable meal.

Her pestle weighs 4 kg and the pounding task
is sweat, toil, time, and energy. It is an effort.
Mortar and pestle are a pair molded
from a tree stump and branch.

Threshing and Shelling

I'm telling you they are serious
They are threshing and shelling

They grow and harvest crops
Tell what, they shell groundnuts

They grow, grind and winnow crops
and dry them in the sun before dehulling

The Grain Song

Lorraine, here's the domain of words slain,
I'm here to entertain, attain, not to feign!
Hop onto the train, you won't sing in vain,
Words can reach a fever pitch in a brain!
in another twist of drama, let me explain,
Grain, you remain her main food and gain
in spite of others' disdain, sprain and pain,
She doesn't consider you as a stain or a chain,
I see her pound you grain, again and again like rain,
What a drain, yet she doesn't refrain or complain.

Come On and Cruise On

a piece proved that poetry
Can be gorgeously poised
and gorged like a delicacy

a viable mode of transportation
It's hale and hearty for the mind
The soul and spirit's medication

and that it can take readers out
of all—out of politics into poetics—
Out of themselves and their spaces

and cruise with them far-off and nigh
into warmth and words and wisdom
On and on till it reaches a cool crescendo

A Landing and a Crescendoing Drone

an insect landed on a helpless hunter
by accident, it was flying, flying
around looking for wooded shrubs
or hardwood trees to land on,
it hoped to cajole a companion
and be cozy a bit and lay eggs
but it winged and leaped on him!
wasn't he dazed or superstitious?
doubtlessly he yelped: damn insect!

meanwhile, in a forested,
grassy expanse, a male one,
with its sucking mouthparts and all,
got the hunter thinking, thinking
of a leafhopper, a plant feeder;
its wings long, transparent,
it made it: a disturbing din,
a loud, shrill droning noise,
the male cicada vibrated
two membranes, yes, two
membranes on its abdomen,
it produced a shrill sound on
the underside of its abdomen,
the hunter heard its clamor
as if it were announcing a dusk
with its sound organ which is
NOT called a cymbal but a tymbal,
an instrumentalist that uses its ribs
to produce its rare jungle jazz music,
so concluded the bushed hunter in the bush

Face-to-Face with a Faceless Face

the sun had rolled and retired
into the cheerful cuddle of its mom,
giving way to a dense dusk to dance,
and nocturnal creatures to creep,
shamble and sing their silly songs,

late, she was stomping and singing
in a bid to give herself a false sense
of fearlessness, freeness and fun,
a hunch herded her to turn around
and take an abrupt look, and Lord!

there was something unfamiliar
about the fast fellow's familiarity,
she couldn't figure out who he was,
but his gaiety appeared like a sight
his eyes were used to slapping on,

but who is he? what is he up to?
is he rushing to catch up with me?
would he not harm me? would he say
hi? would he propose to me? would
he accept a direct or diplomatic snub?

there was an air of awkwardness,
quickness and foreignness about him
that made her hair to stand on end:
who is this long-limbed loose rover?
look at his robotic speed, his lankiness!

if only I had a cheetah
s legs that are longer
and leaner than those of other cats . . . then
I would lift them off the ground and cross them
underneath my body while abounding along!

If a were a horse I would lengthen my stride
and transition from a careful, cute canter
to a faraway, flying and fierce gallop,
if a hole could just heave up and swallow
me up, if I had left home earlier . . . if . . .
if that man had just left me alone . . .

she lamented, labored, reflected;
pondered, prayed as she purred;
was he an alien with a faceless face?
the shadowy lanky loner paced
past her quaking frame without

as much as a care or a sound
along a fine forested footpath,
as a result, a mammoth mass
of gathered firewood fell off
her flighty flummoxed head!

Seeking Refuge

Messages come in many shapes, sizes and colors
but what is crucial is how we interpret and implement them.

If friendships, relationships or marriages
were scripted like plays and movies,
life would not be as dramatic and enigmatic as we know it to be.

We write and practice our scripts as we live, love and transition.
I love the sky. How magic it is to marvel at that celestial dome
as it towers above the Earth.
I begin to visualize daylight and the delight
of sightseeing birds and insects as they fly in their sky.

I bask in the cordiality and cuddle of the sun,
and wander away in a trance into the wonder of the clouds,
    lightning
and rainbows before arriving at the constellations.
I then go clubbing with the night and its stars, and the moon,
(though the stars hog the limelight!)

I love the wilderness in the form of wild animals, forests,
    vegetation,
rocks, rivers and beaches.
These amazingly beautiful things go about their business
despite human intervention. Bravo!

People, the preservation of the universe—
which is the natural, physical, or material world—
is essentially the preservation of life, and this cause is close to my
    heart.

Finally, I decide to hang out
with precious Precipitation's dear family and friends,
I mean lovely and lively chaps like Rain, Hail, Drizzle, Sleet and Snow.
What fun! No company beats their watery warmth, harmonies and hospitality, I swear!!

The Bravery of a Stolen Heart

Bonani traversed beyond the small and big hills
Beyond the singing mountains and valleys

The bushes were full of thorns and roots
and were a well-known refuge for snakes

He braved windy or chilly nights
and the frightening sounds of owls

Whooo whooo whooo whooo
Hoo hoo hoo hoo

Maybe the owls were hooting:
Who cooks for you?

Who cooks for you-all?
Who cooks for you?

Were the witches and wizards
Not stalking him too?

What about the infamous ghost
Over Nkanyezi bridge?
Was it not said to be stubborn?
Was it not said to be talkative and slippery?

Sometimes he heard dogs bark
Sometimes there was some grunting

Jackals howled and snakes hissed
Lions roared but he was undeterred

at times the night's darkness
Was blinding and confusing

But Bonani groped for the path
and rummaged through the bushes

Sometimes the rivers were flooded
Sometimes the rain pounded

For Bonani it was just a delay
He usually reached his destination

His destination kept his heart
Beyond the hills and valleys

Beyond the streams and rivers
Someone had stolen his heart

I Can't Get Enough of It

Please, please
take me there,
Let me lose myself to it,
Let me have a feel, a blast,
Let me tuck into it, not once, not the last!

Please let me loose,
I seek to spoil myself and unwind . . .
until all my woes cannot be seen or found!
Yes, let me voyage and get lost in the warm heart
and embrace and love and loveliness
of the astonishing Matobo National Park!

Fun galore . . .
Nature's bliss mollifies
my soul at the Maleme Dam,
No, I want to go wild and spring
over the giant granite boulders
overlooking the dam.
The reptiles assured me,
they said come and roll,
please come and have a ball.
I have a must-attend meeting with
the gregarious reptiles there too!
On the agenda is fun and fun,
We shall sit on those rocks and
chit-chat. No biting business today!

by the way, I would like to reach
the summit of Malindindzimu,
"the hill of benevolent spirits"
and experience the wonder
Cecil Rhodes called
"View of the World."

The San's rock paintings
will certainly rock and
roll with me.

I am an ever-hungry consumer of
information, so the interpretive museum
at the Pomongwe Caves will come in handy!

Oh, please take me there,
I want to feel home,
I want to feel the majestic African sun
brighten me up. Its rays kiss my face
and forehead with tenderness.

Please accompany me to the Whovi Wild area,
which is home to several bird species
and lots of species of mammals.
Oh, what a sight . . .
Look at the black and white rhinoceros,
the zebra, the giraffe, the antelope, the leopard,
the flat-footed cheetah, the brown hyena.

I am a big fan of guided walks and pony trails.
of course, l will go fishing in some
of the dams in the Matobo National Park
before I disappear into one of those thatched lodges.
I need to slow down, cool down a little. Re-energize.
Tuck into something finger-licking good. Here I know
they serve one with mouth-watering stuff and comfort!

On the following day another paradise
waits for me. The mighty Victoria
Falls! This is Africa, dear. I can't
get enough of this continent's
heavenly tourist centers.

A New Flower

in the foothills of the charming Entoto Mountains
You sprawl as a cute commercial and cultural hub
a New Flower whose anthers are in the millions
You are a Flower whose nectar none can snub!

in historical, diplomatic and political terms—
You are the real deal, talk of Africa's center
The presence of the African Union confirms
Addis Ababa, I see tourists and florists enter!

Safety Regulations Paramount

Is it not time to stand up to carelessness?
Couldn't the harshness or damage of the
leakage have been significantly reduced
or mitigated if they had implemented
basic safety regulations or measures?
an environmental and health catastrophe,
the shady cloud that billows toxic fumes
for months resulting in health, psychological
and ecological challenges, people affected,
poor plants endangered, animals threatened

Little Hills of Esigodini

fabulous sight
landforms snake up and down
in an extraordinary fashion
of Nature's poise and pride
breasts of land projecting
into charged saddles
saddles always midwifed
to gush out milk
of purity and tranquility
the hills though
small in size
short in height
lug and beam
a beauty that towers
the sky of my intrigue
their warmth appendages
the body with a nobility priceless
like a cup of undiluted water
they stand out undisturbed
unchallenged by the ever-jerky
wheels of seasons and weather
during gusty days their music
romances my ears with
a rare calmness
l feel altogether like abandoning
my journey for them
crowning them my beautiful infinity
during sun-drenched days
their seemingly little panorama
drowns and dazzles my eyes into captivity
an image of snug oases
unparalleled greening of my soul
they snuggle me all the way to the apex
of amity and stimulation

they vacillate between ideal and real
l relish to no end
their serrated depressions and passages
that feel me with a passion
beyond mere touch and tour
they captivate my touch at will
l cannot give them a cursory look
the harder l try to scuttle away
the further and so further
l gravitate into their cuddling glare
they confer upon me the throne
of Nature's dutiful and indebted admirer
of the stupendous dexterity of our Creator
the little hills that dominate my dreams
those that epitomize a hustle-free haven
for the breezy incubation and birth
of a romance and a love of a lifetime
those are my little hills
they will define and refine my life
so that l get to appreciate the meaning
of dreams and days

A Thirsty Throat

Won't it die without a drink?
What about a dead beast's stink?
Our land is gasping for great greenery
The one that was a cute castle of scenery
Is now a poor, petrifying, parched plainness
The rains forsook the farmers' hopefulness
When they withdrew and played hide-and-seek
With their patient prayers which are purely meek
That's why our land is lacking and drearily dehydrated
The crops cry dry dirges of drooping, none is exhilarated

Nature Seeks Good Health and Happiness

I hear the stillness of streams,
what can be purer and pinker
than the sincere sight and splash
of our mother nature, the wildlife?
what can be lovelier than its love?

My heart and hands are happy
and healed by graceful gardens
that restore, reign and rave
in my soul, on the horizon,
in the landscape of wonder!

Nature has a way of nurturing
my spirits and planting, pruning
greens of calm in my dizzy, dozy eyes;
I'm fond of fun outings and sightings,
my soul strolls into spaces of the wildlife.

It does so to energize and conscientize
, to preach of the preciousness of flora, fauna;
to poetize about how poems can conceal, conjoin
with the purity and personification of the high sky,
to let its pureness pour out of peace, poetry and people.

I hear the self-defeating, deafening dins of humans,
as if it's not bad to burn fossil fuels, to go on sprees
of bush burning, illegal gold panning, sand winning, logging;
mother nature's health is affected adversely by water pollution,
mother nature's happiness is taken away by acts of deforestation,
there is an odor of toxicity, a sight of impiety, a feel of death,
   decay.

Time to Change Course

it needs more protectors
than pretenders, polluters,
it's pulverized by polluters,
precious planet is pestered,
nature is no longer nurtured,
species are enraged and endangered
for two-thirds of the rainforest is ruined,
human life reduced, the coral reefs halved,
will the look of mass extinction galvanize
the wealthy nations to turn half of the world
into a great, green zone, a reserve for nature?
lovely oceans, rivers and trees scream for care,
please people, the planet has to be protected
from unkind and destructive human activities,
for a wounded natural world is a hurt human life

Transitioning Time

Thembi torches my soul
as she talks and touches
on the imperiled wailing whales,
fuming fisheries, slimy oil spills,
crying communities and ecosystems.

She laments lamentations of the advent
of hurtful heatwaves, of the melting sea ice,
of busy business deals that endanger the safety
of dwindling species, of extreme weather events,
and a capacity for a solar and wind energy transition.

Thembi touches on a touching reality, a nerve center,
I have listened to her pleas, never has the activist said this:
my apologies, populaces, it's pathetic that I cannot provide
you with further information and assistance as your inquiry
lies beyond my jurisdiction of interest, mandate and expertise.

Thembi and other climate change activists are my icons,
She says: tell, tell them to desist from leasing our waters
to oil and gas multinationals, for we have had enough
of the perils associated with climate-shattering fossil fuels,
it's time to transition to 100% clean energy to protect our planet.

Our Lives Are a Tour of Hope

Our lives are rich with history,
cyphers, whispers, woes and wins,
with commonalities and diversities,
with songs, myths and aphorisms.

Our lives are rich with aquatic thirsts,
the tears of joy of the pregnant clouds,
the silent seas, streams and roaring rivers,
dryness pales life yet damp gives it a jab.

Our lives are tactful, careful or clumsy
classrooms and coaches, we are possibly
constant, cautious or uncertain students of life,
we breathe in and out lessons, seasons and reasons.

Our lives are a series of changes, chances and conundrums,
a positive march into the preceding, the present and the coming,
a rough road with dreams, dams, dictates and estates that need
nurturing; and tired, teary trees that need our care, protection.

Our lives are the drums that announce an event or a development,
the tender motherly murmurs of Nature and her seen and unseen
brood, the beautiful, beaming rays of the rising, fresh and far sun,
the dawn of a day and its possibilities, promise and high horizons.

I see a flight of faith, value, valor, chasers of happiness and hopes.
I spot the scope of the sky and feel the finesse of its powerful pitch
as it let loose a tough thunder that leaves my wonder asunder,
in humans, faunas, plants, there is dash of drive, love, loveliness.

It Is Time to Speak Up

in protest of a climate change crisis,
soil degradation, ocean acidification,

species loss, deforestation, pollution,
victims of heatwaves, floods, droughts

and all the life-threatening effects
of this disaster, of this time bomb;

I speak up on behalf of nature,
the environment, the planet.

I speak the language of protection,
I speak in the name of biodiversity,

sustainability, resilience, climate action,
planetary health, happiness and hygiene.

Climate-Connected Conflicts

It is an irrefutable conflict threat multiplier
in more than one way or shape or size or color.

It has the effect of worsening political, social,
economic and cultural tensions and conflicts.

For it escalates cases and situations of water
scarcity, food insecurity and resource competition.

From time to time, it causes conflicts and violence
as displaced groups fight for farming and grazing land.

Environmental conflicts spring up as people's clashing
interests, views and values on land come to the fore.

Climate conflicts happen as populaces differ on public land
use, private land development, waste disposal and hazards.

Climate change is a conflict threat multiplier as it spurs
migration, overexploitation, land degradation and grabbing.

We Are Not Merchants of Doom

Can we have oil and gas development
without pollution and degradation?

Are we peddlers of ecological doom
when we warn of a climate catastrophe?

How beautiful it is to see the budding of new
plant life, animals emerge from hibernation.

How worrying it is to see wildlife imperiled
because of industrial attacks from polluters.

Don't we have the right to clean air and water?
What about not sending chemicals into waterways?

No to Demolishers of Climate Progress

Seeking regeneration, resilience, healing, health,
help, happiness: the tenacity of the human spirit.

Galvanized into climate action, into voting
and voicing a NO to anything harms our climate.

No to bills that seek to repel or weaken
climate strategies and creative programs.

No to those who seek to delay or derail
a transition to clean energy alternatives.

No to those whose actions and policies
do not protect the health of communities.

No to those launch assaults on climate change
progress, clean energy policies and ecological laws.

Why Hilltop Farming Is Not That Rosy

Villagers resorted to hilltop farming in a bid
to escape the droughts, floods and other
uncertainties and effects of climate change.

Unlike their forefathers who farmed downhill,
they claimed that their traditional farmlands'
fertile soil had been washed away the heavy rains.

Unlike their traditional farmlands which had turned
into barren strips, the hilltops had fertile soil cover
by virtue of centuries of decaying organic matter.

The villagers thought that they had accessed fertile land
on the hilltops, but then agriculturists cautioned them
that their joy was brief, hilltop farming is untenable.

They stated that farming uphill tampers with the ecosystem,
and causes less water to trickle downhill, since hills act
as sponges which gently release water into streams.

agricultural extension officers warned villagers
that treeless hilltops poised the risks of floods, soil
erosion and mudslides that could shatter their homes.

The Wild Whirlwind Will Wane

Resting after coming back
from a mind-numbing time:
hoeing and fencing off the field,
she heard the doors bang and squeak,
she heard the doors sulk and shudder.

By virtue of the force of the whirlwind,
paper and leaves soared, sped in the wind,
for the wild whirlwind has a terrible, tumultuous
tendency of stirring up things, of tossing, tucking
away: cash, clothes, belongings, books and stillness.

The whirlwind comes to the party with a host of terrors,
their mission is to stir up emotions, plunge populations
into disquiet, disharmony, destruction and despondency;
the wild whirlwind circled around mom's yard with a fury
that left in its trail an ecological and mental turbulence.

Mom's heart stampeded as she caught sight
of her prized garments lose their clasp of the washing line,
as they somersaulted, protested and plummeted away,
while her blankets and sheets were butted by invisible blows,
by dust and dirt; still the wild whirlwind waned and chilled.

About the Author

 Sibanda is a Bulawayo-born poet, novelist, and nonfiction writer who has a passion for themes and topics around conservation, nature, development and justice. He believes that he is a poet in prose, and hence he has never looked back since building and marching into the very first poetry pharmacy in the world, where poetry . . . and poetry and poetics are the most tonic threesome prescriptions!

Sibanda has received the following nominations: the National Arts Merit awards (NaMa), the Mary Ballard Poetry Chapbook Prize, the Best of the Net Prose and the Pushcart Prize. Sibanda's book *Notes, Themes, Things and Other Things: Confronting Controversies, Contradictions and indoctrinations* was considered for *The 2019 Restless Book Prize for New Immigrant Writing in Nonfiction.* Ndaba's book titled *Cabinet Meetings: of Big and Small Preys* was considered for *The Graywolf Press Africa Prize 2018.* Sibanda is a three-time Pushcart nominee. He can be spotted landscaping, lurking, lounging and even lost on various and many media networks.

www.ingramcontent.com/pod-product-compliance
Lightning Source LLC
Chambersburg PA
CBHW072201160426
43197CB00012B/2473